Sacha Lord

In the heart of Altrincham, Cheshire, a future icon of the British music scene and nightlife was born on January 26, 1972. Sacha John Edward Lord, a child whose early days unfolded in the diverse cultural milieu of Greater Manchester, was destined to leave an indelible mark on the world of music and entertainment.

Early Years: A Prelude to Greatness
Sacha's journey wasn't one of immediate success. The son of a textile merchant and an interior designer, he received his education at Manchester Grammar School. However, academic excellence eluded him, leaving school with grades far from impressive. But little did he know that his real classroom was the vibrant streets of Manchester, and his true lessons were in the realms of music and entrepreneurship.

The Rise of a Music Entrepreneur
Post-school life saw Sacha in the humble beginnings of a clothes shop in Altrincham. His entrepreneurial spirit soon led him to a market stall in Liverpool, selling leather jackets. But it was the magnetic pull of the rave-influenced music scene, echoing the beats of The Stone Roses, Prince, The Smiths, and David Bowie, that truly captured his soul.

The Warehouse Project: A Symphony of Beats

2006 marked a turning point. Alongside co-founder Sam Kandel, Sacha launched the Warehouse Project, a series of rave events that transformed Manchester's music scene. Starting in the old Boddingtons Brewery, this venture was a bold move, with the opening night next to a prison causing more than a little controversy. Yet, the project flourished, attracting names like New Order, The Chemical Brothers, and a then-unknown Calvin Harris, and eventually evolving into the UK's largest club night.

Parklife Festival: The Magnum Opus

Sacha's ambitions soared higher with the creation of the Parklife Festival in 2010. This festival became a musical mecca, drawing in 80,000 visitors annually and hosting legends like Snoop Dogg and Liam Gallagher. Moving from Platt Fields Park to Heaton Park, Parklife not only became a staple of Manchester's culture but also a significant contributor to local causes through the Parklife Community Foundation.

Beyond the Turntables: A Voice for the Night

In 2018, Sacha's influence expanded beyond the dance floor. Appointed as Greater Manchester's Night Time Economy Adviser by Mayor Andy Burnham, he became a pivotal figure in advocating for the sector's safety, transport, and cultural diversity. His voice also resonated in the fight for fair wages for nighttime hospitality staff.

Championing Change Amidst Crisis

The 2020 Coronavirus pandemic saw Sacha emerging as a crucial advocate for the UK nightlife sector. He challenged government policies, fought for the rights of hospitality venues, and raised substantial funds for those impacted in the industry.

Personal Life: A Harmony of Love and Commitment

Sacha's personal life resonated with the same passion he had for his work. In 2022, he married Demi Mclaughlin in a beautiful ceremony in Capri, a testament to his belief in love and companionship amidst challenging times.

Legacy: The Beat Goes On

Today, Sacha Lord stands not just as a music entrepreneur but as a beacon of resilience, innovation, and advocacy in the ever-evolving world of nightlife and entertainment. His journey from a market stall to the pinnacle of Manchester's night economy is a symphony of determination, creativity, and unyielding passion for the power of music and community.

Once upon a time in the quaint town of Altrincham, Cheshire, a boy named Sacha John Edward Lord was born on a frosty morning of January 26, 1972. Little did the world know that this boy, cradled in the arms of a textile merchant and an interior designer, was destined to become the pulsating heart of Britain's nightlife.

As a young lad, Sacha's footsteps echoed through the halls of Manchester Grammar School. Yet, the grades on his report card sung a different tune from the dreams in his heart. With two Us and an E at A-Level, Sacha's academic journey was far from the storybooks. But every hero's journey has its own unique beginning, and Sacha's was no different.

After his school days, Sacha's adventure took him to a clothing shop in Altrincham. But the humdrum of retail could not chain down his entrepreneurial spirit. Soon, he found himself amidst the hustle and bustle of Liverpool market, selling leather jackets. It was a modest start, but the stage was being set for something monumental.

As fate would have it, Sacha's life took a turn when the rave-influenced music scene of Manchester beckoned. Enthralled by the rhythms of The Stone Roses, Prince, The Smiths, and David Bowie, Sacha found his true calling. The music wasn't just sound to his ears; it was the beat of his future.

In 2006, like a phoenix rising from the ashes, Sacha, along with his comrade Sam Kandel, birthed The Warehouse Project. What began in the abandoned Boddingtons Brewery and under the arches of Manchester Piccadilly station, soon became a legend. The opening night was not without its challenges, stirring even the prisoners nearby. But like all great tales, the project soared, drawing in crowds by the thousands and artists of the highest calibre.

But Sacha's ambition knew no bounds. He spread his wings further and in 2010, Parklife Festival was born. This wasn't just a festival; it was a cultural phenomenon. From the green expanses of Platt Fields Park to the vastness of Heaton Park, Parklife became a sanctuary for music lovers, with stars like Snoop Dogg and Liam Gallagher gracing its stages.

Meanwhile, Sacha's influence seeped beyond the realms of music. In 2018, he stepped into a new role as Greater Manchester's Night Time Economy Adviser. His was a voice for the voiceless, fighting for safer nights, fair wages, and inclusivity. He wasn't just shaping the nightlife; he was safeguarding it.

Then came the trials of the 2020 pandemic, a tempest that threatened to drown the night he had so passionately built. But like a true hero, Sacha stood firm, challenging policies, protecting the vulnerable, and raising funds to keep the spirit of nightlife alive.

Amidst this maelstrom, Sacha found his harbor in Demi Mclaughlin, marrying her in a romantic ceremony in Capri in 2022. It was a union that celebrated love and resilience, proving that even in the darkest times, there is light.

Now, as we turn the pages of Sacha Lord's story, we see more than a music entrepreneur; we see a visionary, a warrior for the night, a beacon of hope. His tale is a reminder that from the humble beginnings of a market stall can rise a legend, one who not only dances to the beat of his own drum but also orchestrates a symphony for a city, and indeed, for an entire generation.

In the heart of Manchester, as the city lights twinkle like stars in an urban sky, Sacha's journey continues to unfold, each chapter more vibrant than the last. His story, interwoven with the fabric of the city's nightlife, becomes a tapestry of resilience, innovation, and passion.

Sacha's venture into the world of football, as the chairman of Wythenshawe F.C., adds yet another dimension to his multifaceted life. In the roaring stands and on the lush green fields, he finds a new community to uplift, a new dream to nurture. Under his guidance, the club, much like his festivals, becomes a beacon of local spirit and pride, a gathering place for people from all walks of life.

As a staunch advocate for drug safety at music events, Sacha's voice becomes louder and more influential. He isn't just an orchestrator of festivals and events; he is a guardian of those who attend them. His efforts in promoting drug testing labs and on-site forensic testing become a crusade to ensure that every beat and melody is enjoyed in safety and wellness.

But the dance of Sacha's life is not just about grand events and public campaigns. It's in the quiet moments too, in his support for mental health services, especially for those who live their lives in the night time economy. He understands that behind the vibrant façade of the nightlife are real people with real struggles, and he extends his hand in solidarity and support.

The tale of Sacha Lord is not just one of success and achievement; it is a saga of transformation and impact. From the streets of Altrincham to the grand stages of Parklife, from the boardrooms discussing policies to the intimate moments of charitable work, his journey is a testament to the power of dreams and the impact one individual can have on the world around them.

As the story of Sacha Lord continues to be written, with each new challenge and opportunity, one thing remains clear: he is not just creating events or advising on policies; he is crafting a legacy. A legacy that will echo through the streets of Manchester and beyond, inspiring future generations to dream big, to fight for what they believe in, and to always dance to the music of their hearts.

And so, as the night falls over Manchester, and the music from The Warehouse Project fills the air, we know that Sacha's story is far from over. It is a story that will be told and retold, a story of a boy from Altrincham who became the king of Manchester's nightlife, a story of a man who built his dreams into reality, and in doing so, became a legend.

As the pages of Sacha's story turn, his influence in the world of football with Wythenshawe F.C. echoes the same spirit of community and excellence that defines his ventures in the music industry. He isn't just the chairman of a football club; he becomes a pillar of hope and ambition for the team and its supporters. Under his leadership, the club not only plays the game but also plays a pivotal role in the community, fostering local talent and bringing people together in a shared passion for the sport.

Sacha's journey, however, is not without its trials. The advent of the Coronavirus pandemic presents a formidable challenge, a storm that threatens the very essence of the communal and celebratory worlds he has helped cultivate. Yet, in these trying times, his resilience shines brightest. As the night life sector reels under the weight of lockdowns and restrictions, Sacha emerges as a beacon of advocacy and support. His legal battles against the government's curfew policies and the closure of indoor hospitality are not just fights for his interests but battles fought for the entire industry. He stands not only as a businessman but as a champion for the countless individuals whose livelihoods depend on the night time economy.

In these moments of crisis, Sacha's commitment to charity and community welfare takes on a new urgency. His work with the UnitedWeStream Manchester campaign demonstrates his ability to innovate in the face of adversity, transforming the challenge into an opportunity for unity and support. The campaign, a blend of music and philanthropy, not only provides a platform for artists but also becomes a lifeline for those affected by the pandemic, exemplifying the power of community in times of need.

Personal joy also finds its way into Sacha's life amidst these turbulent times. His marriage to Demi Mclaughlin in the picturesque island of Capri is a celebration of love, a reminder of the beauty and joy that life has to offer even in the most challenging times. Their union is a testament to the enduring power of love and partnership.

As the story of Sacha Lord unfolds, it becomes clear that his life is more than a series of events and achievements. It is a journey of impact and inspiration. From the bustling night clubs to the echoing football fields, from the high courts of justice to the quiet acts of charity, Sacha weaves a narrative of relentless passion and unwavering commitment to his community.

The tale of Sacha Lord is a reminder that one person's vision and determination can ignite change, inspire others, and make a lasting difference in the world. His story is not just a chronicle of personal success; it's a narrative of how passion, when coupled with purpose and perseverance, can create a legacy that resonates across communities and generations.

As the music fades into the night and the cheers of the football fans echo in the distance, Sacha's journey continues, a relentless dance of dreams, challenges, and triumphs. His story, ever-evolving and dynamic, is a testament to the enduring spirit of humanity and the transformative power of following one's heart.

As the narrative of Sacha Lord's life unfolds, it transcends the boundaries of a mere success story, evolving into a tapestry rich with the hues of innovation, resilience, and community spirit. Each chapter of his journey, be it in the electrifying realms of music festivals or the grassroots level of football, resonates with a deeper purpose — to enrich, to empower, and to entertain.

In the bustling streets of Manchester, Sacha's influence as the Night Time Economy Adviser for Greater Manchester becomes increasingly evident. His role, far from being a ceremonial title, is a testament to his commitment to the city's vibrant nightlife. His recommendations for improving safety, transport, and cultural diversity are not just policies but lifelines that help sustain and nurture the very heart of the city's culture. Under his guidance, Manchester's nights pulsate with life, offering safe havens for enjoyment and expression.

However, Sacha's journey is not without its hurdles. The global pandemic, which brought unprecedented challenges, also served as a crucible for his leadership and vision. His fight against restrictive policies, while rooted in the present, also speaks to a larger narrative of resistance — a resistance against measures that inadvertently stifle the communal and celebratory spirit of society. His legal battles and advocacy during these times are emblematic of a leader who is not afraid to confront giants for the greater good.

Yet, amidst these battles, Sacha's heart beats in unison with the pulse of the community. His role in the Joshua Wilson Brain Tumour Charity and his advocacy for mental health services, especially in the night time economy, reveal a softer, yet equally powerful side of his character. These efforts showcase a man deeply aware of his social responsibilities, striving to extend his support beyond the glitz of nightlife and into the more profound corners of human needs and welfare.

In his personal life, Sacha's marriage to Demi Mclaughlin is not just a romantic union but a symbol of resilience and hope. Their delayed wedding, a consequence of the pandemic, becomes a celebration that transcends the challenges of the times, symbolizing the enduring nature of love and companionship.

As the story of Sacha Lord continues to unfold, it becomes a narrative not just of one man's journey but of a larger movement. It's a story about how passion, when channeled through the veins of business, advocacy, and charity, can become a powerful force for change. Sacha's life becomes a mirror reflecting the potential within each person to impact their community and beyond.

His legacy, etched in the heartbeats of rave music, the cheers of football fans, and the grateful smiles of those he's helped, is a testament to the fact that life is not just about the heights one reaches but the lives one touches along the way. Sacha Lord's story is a beacon, illuminating a path where dreams, no matter how bold, can be pursued with relentless passion and a deep sense of purpose.

As the pages of Sacha Lord's story turn, they reveal a man who deftly juggles the vibrancy of his professional endeavors with the richness of his personal commitments. In his role as the chairman of Wythenshawe F.C., Sacha embarks on a new chapter, blending his love for music and nightlife with the grassroots passion of football. This venture is more than a business proposition; it's a heartfelt pledge to the community, a commitment to nurturing local talent and fostering a spirit of unity and pride within the team and its supporters.

This narrative takes an intriguing twist as Sacha, a man synonymous with the pulsating energy of nightclubs and festivals, steps into the world of football. His unique perspective, shaped by years of orchestrating some of the most iconic music events, brings a fresh dynamism to the club. Under his stewardship, Wythenshawe F.C. is not just a football team; it becomes a symbol of communal strength, a beacon of local pride that galvanizes the community in new, exhilarating ways.

Meanwhile, Sacha's influence as a music entrepreneur continues to reverberate across the globe. From the immersive experiences of The Warehouse Project to the eclectic beats of Parklife Festival, his creations are more than events; they are cultural phenomena that capture the essence of a generation. These festivals, known for their diverse line-ups and inclusive atmospheres, are a reflection of Sacha's vision — a world where music is a unifying force, transcending boundaries and bringing people together in celebration of life and artistry.

In this unfolding tale, Sacha's role during the coronavirus pandemic emerges as a defining moment. His staunch advocacy and legal challenges against government restrictions highlight a leader willing to stand up for his industry's survival. These actions paint the picture of a man deeply connected to his roots, fiercely protective of his community, and unafraid to challenge the status quo to safeguard the interests of the many who depend on the nightlife sector for their livelihood.

Through the narrative weave moments of personal triumph and resilience. Sacha's wedding to Demi Mclaughlin, a celebration delayed but undiminished by the pandemic, stands as a poignant reminder of the enduring power of love and partnership. This chapter in his life story adds a layer of depth to his character, revealing a man who values the sanctity of personal commitments as much as his professional ones.

As the story of Sacha Lord continues to unfold, it becomes clear that his life is more than a series of successful ventures. It is a journey marked by a relentless pursuit of innovation, a deep commitment to community, and an unwavering dedication to creating spaces where joy, music, and togetherness can thrive. In every role he takes on, Sacha leaves an indelible mark, not just as a visionary entrepreneur, but as a catalyst for change and a beacon of hope, inspiring others to dream big and work tirelessly towards turning those dreams into reality.

In the grand tapestry of his life, each thread — from his early struggles to his towering achievements — weaves together a narrative that is as inspiring as it is instructive. Sacha Lord's story stands as a testament to the power of resilience, the beauty of innovation, and the transformative impact one individual can have on their community and beyond.

As the tale of Sacha Lord unravels further, it reveals a man constantly evolving, not just as a business magnate but as a beacon of societal change. His appointment as Greater Manchester's first Night Time Economy Adviser by Mayor Andy Burnham marks a significant milestone in his journey. Here, Sacha's story takes on a hue of advocacy and altruism. He embraces this role not for monetary gain but for the chance to shape policy and make a tangible difference in the lives of those who form the backbone of the night-time economy.

In this chapter, Sacha emerges as a crusader for fairness and inclusivity. He advocates for safer nightlife spaces, champions the cause of workers' rights, and pushes for initiatives that foster cultural diversity. His recommendations for extended opening hours and improved night-time transport links reflect a deep understanding of the ecosystem he is part of. This role isn't just a title; it's a platform for Sacha to amplify the voices of an often-overlooked community, ensuring they are heard in the corridors of power.

The narrative takes a dramatic turn with the onset of the Coronavirus pandemic. Sacha, a figurehead in the nightlife sector, finds himself at the forefront of an unprecedented crisis. He transforms into a pivotal character, leading the charge to support an industry brought to its knees by lockdowns and restrictions. His legal challenges against the government's policies underscore his unwavering commitment to the sector's survival and the livelihoods of those it supports. These actions paint Sacha not just as a business leader, but as a guardian of an entire cultural sector.

Yet, even in the midst of this turmoil, Sacha's story is punctuated with moments of profound impact and compassion. His co-founding of the UnitedWeStream Manchester campaign during the pandemic adds a layer of philanthropy to his character. This initiative, which raises significant funds for struggling businesses and charities, showcases a leader who is quick to respond to crises with innovative solutions that benefit the wider community.

As the narrative progresses, it delves into the personal realm, revealing facets of Sacha's life that resonate with warmth and humanity. His marriage to Demi Mclaughlin, a beacon of love amidst the challenges of the pandemic, adds a dimension of personal fulfillment to his story. It's a testament to the balance he maintains between his soaring professional life and the nurturing of his personal relationships.

The story of Sacha Lord, as it stands, is a tapestry of triumphs and trials, innovations and initiatives, personal joys, and public duties. Each chapter of his life is a lesson in resilience, a showcase of creativity, and a proof of his commitment to bettering the world around him. His journey is far from over; each day adds a new layer to his legacy, ensuring that his impact will be felt for generations to come. Sacha's life story, rich in its achievements and profound in its influence, continues to inspire and shape the world of music, nightlife, and beyond.

As the narrative of Sacha Lord's life unfolds, it becomes evident that his impact stretches far beyond the confines of nightclubs and music festivals. His story, rich with layers of innovation, advocacy, and personal growth, reveals a man deeply intertwined with the cultural and social fabric of his community.

Amidst the throes of the pandemic, Sacha's role as a defender and savior of the nightlife industry becomes more pronounced. His legal battles against restrictive government policies are not just about keeping doors open; they are a fight for the survival of an entire cultural sector and the livelihoods it supports. His actions resonate deeply with those whose lives are anchored in the night-time economy, painting him as a hero in their eyes.

But Sacha's influence doesn't stop at the courtroom steps. He becomes a vocal advocate for drug safety at music events, championing initiatives that could save lives. This shift from business mogul to public health advocate adds a new dimension to his character, showcasing a commitment to the well-being of his community that transcends financial interests.

In the realm of public service, Sacha continues to shine. His recommendations as Greater Manchester's Night Time Economy Adviser reflect a vision that is both pragmatic and progressive. He pushes for policies that not only support the industry but also ensure its integration into the wider societal fabric. His efforts to improve safety, transport, and accessibility during the night echo a deep understanding of urban dynamics and a genuine concern for the city's residents.

Sacha's story, however, is not just about public victories and professional achievements. It's also deeply personal and human. His marriage to Demi Mclaughlin stands as a testament to the enduring strength of personal relationships, even in times of crisis. This chapter in his life brings a sense of balance and fulfillment, a reminder that behind the public persona lies a man who values love, family, and personal connections.

As the narrative draws to a close, it's clear that Sacha Lord's story is far from over. His journey continues to evolve, marked by a relentless pursuit of innovation, a deep commitment to social responsibility, and an unyielding passion for the nightlife and music industries. His legacy, already substantial, promises to grow even further, driven by a vision that extends well beyond the boundaries of his own enterprises.

Sacha's life is a mosaic of challenges met, battles fought, and victories won, all woven together by a thread of unshakeable determination and a heart firmly rooted in his community. His story, a blend of entrepreneurship, advocacy, and personal journey, stands as a beacon of inspiration, a testament to the power of vision, and the impact one individual can have on the world around them.

The story of Sacha Lord, a tale of triumphs and challenges, now takes a new turn as he embarks on his latest endeavor – revitalizing Wythenshawe F.C. as its chairman. His appointment is more than a mere title; it's a commitment to the community, a chance to infuse his entrepreneurial spirit into the local sports scene. Under his guidance, the football club begins to mirror the vibrancy and success of his other ventures, becoming a symbol of hope and revival in the area.

In parallel, his charitable work continues to shine. As the patron of the Joshua Wilson Brain Tumour Charity, Sacha's influence extends beyond the night-time economy into realms of profound social impact. His commitment to mental health services for those in the nightlife industry further underscores his understanding that a thriving business sector must also nurture the well-being of its participants.

As the world emerges from the shadow of the pandemic, Sacha's role becomes even more crucial. He is at the forefront of rebuilding and reimagining an industry that has been profoundly affected. His insights and leadership guide the sector through uncharted waters, balancing the need for economic recovery with the imperative of public health and safety.

Sacha's life story, filled with its share of ups and downs, becomes a beacon for resilience and adaptation. His journey from a young man selling leather jackets to a prominent figure in the music and nightlife scene is a narrative of transformation, driven by passion and an unyielding will to succeed.

In his personal life, Sacha's marriage to Demi Mclaughlin stands as a sanctuary amid the whirlwind of his professional endeavors. Their relationship, having withstood the trials of postponement due to the pandemic, emerges stronger, symbolizing hope and continuity.

As the chapters of Sacha Lord's life continue to unfold, his legacy is etched not only in the annals of the music and nightlife industries but also in the hearts of those he's touched. His story, a blend of ambition, advocacy, and authenticity, continues to inspire, reminding us that the power to effect change lies within each of us, waiting to be unleashed.

Sacha's journey is a testament to the power of dreams, determination, and dedication. It's a narrative that resonates with anyone who dares to envision a better future, not just for themselves but for the community at large. As he moves forward, the world watches, eager to see the next chapter in the extraordinary saga of Sacha Lord.

As Sacha Lord's story continues, he finds himself at a crossroads, one where his personal passions intersect with his professional pursuits. The challenge of balancing his responsibilities as the chairman of Wythenshawe F.C., his duties as a music entrepreneur, and his role as Greater Manchester's Night Time Economy Adviser, is immense. Yet, Sacha navigates these with a grace born of experience and a resilience forged in the fires of past trials.

Wythenshawe F.C. begins to reflect Sacha's ethos, transforming into a club that not only plays football but also embodies community spirit and social responsibility. Under his stewardship, the club becomes more than a sports team; it turns into a beacon of community engagement and local pride.

Simultaneously, Sacha's influence in the music industry continues to grow. The Warehouse Project and Parklife Festival, already landmarks in the UK's music scene, evolve under his guidance, adapting to the post-pandemic world with innovation and a renewed commitment to safety and inclusivity. These events, emblematic of Sacha's vision, become more than just music festivals; they are cultural phenomena that celebrate diversity, creativity, and unity.

In his role as Greater Manchester's Night Time Economy Adviser, Sacha becomes a pivotal figure in reshaping the region's nightlife. His recommendations lead to significant improvements in safety, transport, and cultural diversity, making Manchester's night-time economy more accessible and vibrant. His advocacy for fair wages and better working conditions elevates the standards of the hospitality industry, benefiting countless workers.

Sacha's personal life, meanwhile, remains a source of strength and stability. His marriage to Demi is a testament to the power of partnership and mutual support. Together, they navigate the complexities of life in the public eye, balancing their professional commitments with the demands of their personal lives.

As Sacha moves forward, his story becomes not just one of individual success, but of community impact. His initiatives, both in the music industry and in the football club, create ripples that extend far beyond their immediate realms. He becomes a symbol of what can be achieved when passion is paired with purpose, and when a visionary leader dedicates himself to the service of his community.

Sacha Lord's story, ever-evolving, is a narrative of transformation. It speaks to the power of dreaming big, the importance of relentless perseverance, and the impact one individual can have on the lives of many. His journey, still unfolding, continues to inspire and challenge, reminding us all that with vision and hard work, anything is possible.

As the chapters of Sacha Lord's life unfold, his influence in the realms of music, sports, and public service coalesces into a legacy of enduring impact. His journey is not just a testament to his own achievements but also a blueprint for how passion and dedication can drive meaningful change.

Within the pulsating heart of Manchester's night-time economy, Sacha's initiatives begin to bear fruit. The city's nightlife scene, rejuvenated under his advisement, becomes a model for other cities. His push for safer, more inclusive, and vibrant night-time experiences transforms Manchester into a magnet for tourists and locals alike, while also ensuring that the welfare of those who work in the industry is never compromised.

At the same time, Sacha's stewardship of Wythenshawe F.C. sees the club ascending not just in league standings but in its role within the community. The club becomes synonymous with local empowerment, fostering youth programs and community outreach initiatives that extend beyond the football pitch. Under Sacha's guidance, the club becomes more than a team; it becomes a symbol of hope and unity.

In the world of music, The Warehouse Project and Parklife Festival continue to evolve, adapting to the changing landscapes of music and society. These events, under Sacha's visionary leadership, become more than just entertainment venues. They transform into platforms for social change, promoting environmental sustainability, drug safety, and mental health awareness, reflecting Sacha's deep commitment to the well-being of his patrons.

Meanwhile, Sacha's personal life is a quiet harbor amid his professional endeavors. His marriage with Demi remains a source of strength and joy, a private sanctuary that nourishes and rejuvenates him. Their partnership, rooted in mutual respect and understanding, stands as a testament to the power of love and support in navigating the complexities of life in the limelight.

Sacha's story, rich with triumphs and challenges, is a beacon of inspiration. It serves as a reminder that one's work can transcend personal achievement and become a catalyst for widespread positive change. His journey is a vivid illustration of how dedication, creativity, and a deep commitment to one's community can create a lasting legacy that reshapes industries, uplifts communities, and touches countless lives.

As Sacha Lord continues to write his story, the pages are filled with the promise of more achievements, more challenges, and an enduring commitment to making a difference. His life, a tapestry of passion, perseverance, and purpose, continues to inspire and influence, echoing the timeless truth that with vision, hard work, and a heart for service, one can indeed leave an indelible mark on the world.

The narrative of Sacha Lord's life unfolds like a grand tapestry, woven with threads of innovation, community service, and personal fulfillment. As he steps into the future, his vision for a more vibrant and inclusive night-time economy in Greater Manchester continues to evolve.

Sacha's role as a Night Time Economy Adviser, though challenging, becomes increasingly pivotal. He pioneers groundbreaking initiatives, advocating for the rights and well-being of workers in the hospitality sector. His efforts lead to improved working conditions, fair wages, and a stronger sense of community among those who keep the city's nightlife vibrant and alive.

Simultaneously, Sacha's influence in the music world reaches new heights. The Warehouse Project and Parklife Festival, jewels in Manchester's cultural crown, grow in prestige under his stewardship. These events become more than mere entertainment; they are crucibles of cultural exchange and innovation. Under Sacha's guidance, they champion environmental sustainability, setting new standards in the industry. He introduces initiatives like waste reduction programs and sustainable energy sources, proving that large-scale events can be both exhilarating and environmentally responsible.

In his role with Wythenshawe F.C., Sacha brings a sense of unity and pride to the local community. He nurtures young talent, providing opportunities for aspiring athletes in the region. The club becomes a beacon of hope and a symbol of the transformative power of sports. Under his leadership, Wythenshawe F.C. not only climbs in rankings but also in the hearts of its supporters.

On a personal front, Sacha's life with Demi continues to be a source of stability and happiness. They share a deep bond, grounded in shared values and mutual respect. Their partnership, away from the public eye, is a testament to the strength that comes from love and companionship.

As the world navigates the post-pandemic era, Sacha becomes an even more influential figure. His experiences during the crisis have equipped him with unique insights into the resilience and adaptability of the night-time economy. He shares these insights on global platforms, inspiring other cities to rethink and rejuvenate their own nightlife sectors.

Sacha's story is not just a chronicle of personal achievement; it's a narrative about the power of community, resilience, and innovation. His journey illustrates how one individual's passion and dedication can ignite change, inspire others, and make a lasting impact on society.

As the chapters of his life continue to unfold, Sacha Lord's legacy grows ever more significant. His story is a beacon for future generations, a testament to the fact that with vision, determination, and a heart for public service, one can indeed make a profound difference in the world.

Sacha Lord's journey, much like the pulsating beats of the music that defined his career, continues to resonate with energy and purpose. His influence extends beyond the dance floors and football fields, seeping into the very fabric of Greater Manchester's night-time economy.

His advocacy for drug safety, born from personal experiences and tragedies within the club scene, becomes a cornerstone of his legacy. Sacha spearheads campaigns for on-site drug testing at festivals and clubs, transforming the nightlife landscape into a safer environment for revelers. This initiative not only saves lives but also shifts the public discourse on drug use and harm reduction.

The coronavirus pandemic, a tumultuous period for many, especially in the hospitality and entertainment sectors, highlights Sacha's leadership qualities. He emerges as a vocal and steadfast champion for the industry, navigating the storm with a blend of pragmatism and optimism. His legal battles against restrictive government policies are not just fights for survival but are emblematic of his deep-seated belief in justice and equity. These efforts solidify his reputation as a protector of the nightlife community, earning him both respect and admiration from peers and government officials alike.

In his personal life, Sacha's marriage to Demi Mclaughlin becomes a haven of support and love. Together, they navigate the complexities of a life lived in the public eye, finding solace in each other's company. Their relationship, while private, serves as a subtle reminder of the importance of balance and grounding amid the whirlwind of a public life.

As he moves forward, Sacha's vision for a more inclusive and vibrant night-time economy continues to evolve. He works tirelessly to ensure that Manchester's nightlife is not just a space for entertainment but a platform for cultural expression and social cohesion. His initiatives to improve transport and safety in the night-time economy make the city's nightlife more accessible and enjoyable for all, reflecting his deep commitment to community and inclusivity.

In a world that is constantly changing, Sacha Lord remains a figure of stability and innovation. His story, a blend of personal triumphs and professional milestones, continues to inspire those who dream of making a difference. As he writes new chapters in his remarkable journey, Sacha's legacy as a visionary, a community leader, and a compassionate human being only grows stronger, echoing in the hearts and minds of those whose lives he has touched.

The narrative of Sacha Lord, marked by both grandeur and grit, takes on new dimensions as he delves into the realm of public life. Appointed as Greater Manchester's first Night Time Economy Adviser by Mayor Andy Burnham, Sacha embraces a role that seems tailor-made for him. His expertise, born from years on the front lines of the nightlife sector, becomes instrumental in shaping policies and initiatives. His recommendations, aimed at enhancing safety, transport, and cultural diversity, are not just proposals on paper but are imbued with his personal experiences and deep understanding of the industry.

Sacha's advocacy doesn't stop at the doorsteps of nightclubs and festivals. He takes a firm stand on issues of fair wages and transparency in tipping for hospitality staff, championing the rights of those who are often the backbone of the night-time economy but seldom heard. His efforts to create a more equitable and just environment for workers underscore his commitment to fairness and his belief in the dignity of all forms of labor.

The pandemic, a crucible of challenge and change, further cements Sacha's role as a pivotal figure in the UK's nightlife narrative. His legal battles against government restrictions are not just about reopening doors but are a fight for the very soul of the industry. His outspoken criticism of policies he views as unfair or nonsensical resonates with many, turning him into a beacon of hope and resistance for the beleaguered sector.

In parallel, Sacha's charitable endeavors paint him as a figure of compassion and community spirit. His involvement with the Joshua Wilson Brain Tumour Charity and his efforts to promote mental health awareness in the nightlife sector reflect his understanding that behind the music and the merrymaking, there are real people with real struggles. The success of the UnitedWeStream Manchester campaign, raising significant funds for those affected by the pandemic, is a testament to his ability to mobilize support for a cause greater than himself.

Yet, amidst the public accolades and achievements, Sacha's story remains deeply personal. His marriage to Demi Mclaughlin stands as a testament to the power of love and partnership. Together, they navigate the complexities of life in the limelight, their bond strengthened by shared challenges and triumphs.

As the future unfolds, Sacha Lord's story continues to be written. His journey, marked by resilience, innovation, and a relentless drive to improve the world around him, serves as an inspiration. For those who follow in his footsteps, Sacha's life is a reminder that passion, when coupled with purpose, can lead to extraordinary achievements. His legacy is not just in the festivals he co-created or the campaigns he championed, but in the countless lives he touched and the vibrant, inclusive future he envisions for Manchester's night-time economy.

As Sacha Lord's journey continues, he becomes more than a figure in the nightlife scene; he evolves into a symbol of resilience and innovation in the face of adversity. His relentless pursuit of bettering the night-time economy extends beyond Manchester, influencing policy and practices across the UK. His voice becomes a beacon, guiding the industry through turbulent times, embodying the spirit of a sector that refuses to be silenced.

Sacha's impact is felt not just in the clamor of crowded dance floors or the hum of busy bars, but also in quieter, more profound ways. His work in championing mental health causes, particularly within the high-pressure environment of nightlife, shines a light on often-ignored issues. His advocacy brings hope and support to those who struggle in silence, making the night-time economy a safer and more inclusive space for everyone.

The story of Sacha Lord is also one of transformation and adaptation. As the world changes, so does he, constantly seeking new ways to innovate and improve. His ability to foresee trends and adapt to emerging challenges keeps him at the forefront of the industry. From embracing digital platforms to advocating for sustainable practices, Sacha's vision for the future of nightlife is as dynamic as it is inclusive.

In his personal life, Sacha's marriage to Demi Mclaughlin remains a source of strength and stability. Their partnership, forged in the midst of a global crisis, stands as a testament to the power of love and commitment. Together, they navigate the complexities of a life lived in the public eye, finding joy in shared successes and comfort in each other's support.

As Sacha continues to write his story, his legacy takes on a multifaceted hue. He is not just a music entrepreneur or a night-time economy adviser; he is a visionary, a champion for the underrepresented, and a catalyst for change. His life story, rich with challenges overcome and successes achieved, serves as an inspiration to aspiring entrepreneurs and activists alike. It reminds us that with passion, resilience, and a commitment to making a difference, one can not only dream of a better world but also play a pivotal role in shaping it.

The narrative of Sacha Lord, while rooted in the realms of music and nightlife, transcends these boundaries to tell a universal story of hope, perseverance, and the enduring power of community. As the future unfolds, his journey will undoubtedly continue to inspire, influence, and ignite change, resonating with generations to come.

Sacha's story, as it unfolds, becomes a tapestry of innovation, community, and resilience. His vision for the night-time economy, once a dream born in the vibrant streets and clubs of Manchester, now influences cities and communities far beyond. He becomes a mentor and a guide, sharing his insights and experiences with young entrepreneurs and dreamers who see in him a model of success and social responsibility.

In the ever-evolving landscape of music and nightlife, Sacha remains a step ahead, always anticipating the next trend, the next big challenge. His ability to adapt and innovate becomes legendary. Whether it's leveraging new technologies to enhance the festival experience or finding creative solutions to keep the industry afloat during times of crisis, Sacha's ingenuity knows no bounds.

His work with Wythenshawe F.C. reflects another dimension of his commitment to community. As chairman, he doesn't just see a football club; he sees a heartbeat of a community, a source of local pride and unity. His leadership extends beyond the pitch, fostering a sense of belonging and togetherness, using sports as a vehicle for positive change.

Throughout his journey, Sacha's charitable endeavors continue to grow. His influence helps to raise significant funds for various causes, from brain tumour research to supporting those impacted by the night-time economy. His passion for these causes is infectious, inspiring others to join in and make a difference.

As he moves through life, Sacha's role as Greater Manchester's Night Time Economy Adviser evolves into something more profound. He becomes an advocate for the entire region, a voice for its people and its diverse cultures. His recommendations and initiatives help shape a more vibrant, safe, and inclusive night-time economy, benefiting not just those who work and play in it, but the broader community as well.

Sacha's personal life, too, flourishes. His marriage with Demi becomes a symbol of partnership and mutual support. Together, they navigate the complexities of a life in the public eye, balancing professional endeavors with personal moments of joy and reflection.

As the world watches, Sacha Lord's story continues to be written. It's a story of a man who, with every beat of the music and every challenge faced, reshapes the world around him. He is more than a music entrepreneur or an adviser; he is a beacon of hope, a catalyst for change, and a testament to the power of unwavering dedication and passion.

And so, Sacha's journey continues, a journey not just of a man but of a community, a culture, and a night-time economy that he helped transform. His legacy, etched in the hearts and minds of those he has touched, continues to inspire and influence, a melody that resonates across generations, echoing the timeless rhythm of resilience, innovation, and unity.

The story of Sacha Lord, a man who transformed the night, continues to evolve and inspire. As he steps into the future, his life becomes a beacon of entrepreneurial spirit and social responsibility. Sacha's contributions to the music and nightlife industries are not just about creating spaces for enjoyment but also about fostering communities and nurturing talent.

His role as the Night Time Economy Adviser for Greater Manchester sees him advocating not just for businesses, but for the soul of the city. He understands that the night-time economy is a tapestry of culture, art, and social interaction. Sacha's initiatives lead to safer, more inclusive, and thriving nightlife scenes. His work ensures that the vibrant nightlife continues to be the heartbeat of the city, accessible and enjoyable for all.

Sacha's influence extends to the global stage as well. His successful ventures, like The Warehouse Project and Parklife Festival, become case studies in innovation and excellence, inspiring similar projects worldwide. He speaks at international conferences, sharing his knowledge and experiences, and in doing so, shaping the global discourse on nightlife and community building.

At Wythenshawe F.C., Sacha's impact is palpable. He transforms the club into more than just a football team; it becomes a symbol of community pride and aspiration. Under his guidance, the club not only achieves sporting success but also becomes a hub for community activities, bringing people together and fostering a sense of belonging and local pride.

In his charitable endeavors, Sacha's passion and commitment continue to make a significant impact. His efforts help raise awareness and funds for crucial causes, from mental health support in the nightlife industry to life-saving medical research. He becomes known as much for his philanthropy as for his business acumen.

Sacha's personal life remains a cornerstone of his strength and stability. His marriage to Demi is a partnership that underpins his success. Together, they navigate the complexities of life in the limelight, maintaining a private sanctuary amid public responsibilities. Their love story adds a personal dimension to Sacha's public persona, showcasing the balance between personal fulfillment and professional achievement.

As years go by, Sacha's legacy continues to grow. He is not just remembered as a pioneer in the music and nightlife industry but as a visionary who understood the power of community and culture. His life story becomes a source of inspiration for future generations, a tale of a man who danced to the beat of his own drum and, in doing so, changed the rhythm of the world around him.

Sacha Lord's journey is a testament to the power of passion, resilience, and commitment to one's community. His story is not just about the nights he transformed but about the days he inspired, a narrative of a man who brought light to the darkness, rhythm to the silence, and unity to the community. And so, the beat goes on, with Sacha's legacy continuing to pulse in the heart of every festival beat, in every cheer at Wythenshawe F.C., and in the thriving night streets of Manchester, echoing into eternity.

As Sacha Lord's journey unfolds, his influence in the realm of public policy and community engagement grows stronger. With his deep understanding of the night-time economy, he becomes a key figure in shaping policies that balance the needs of businesses, residents, and cultural communities. His innovative ideas and bold approaches set new standards in city planning and nightlife management, influencing cities beyond Manchester.

His advocacy for fair wages and safe working conditions in the hospitality industry leads to significant reforms. Sacha's voice becomes a powerful catalyst for change, pushing for legislation that ensures the well-being of thousands of workers. His efforts contribute to a more ethical and sustainable hospitality sector, where workers' rights are respected and their contributions valued.

Meanwhile, Sacha's commitment to drug safety and harm reduction at music events becomes a model for festivals and clubs worldwide. His campaign for onsite drug testing and education programs receives international recognition, saving lives and promoting a safer party culture. This initiative not only changes the face of nightlife safety but also starts important conversations about drug policy and public health.

In the world of sports, Sacha's leadership at Wythenshawe F.C. leads to a golden era for the club. His vision extends beyond the pitch; he invests in youth programs, community engagement, and facilities improvement, turning the club into a symbol of hope and progress for the local community. Under his guidance, Wythenshawe F.C. becomes more than just a football club; it becomes a beacon of positive change and community spirit.

Sacha's personal life, too, remains a source of strength and inspiration. His marriage to Demi is a partnership that flourishes amidst their busy lives, a testament to their love and mutual support. Together, they navigate the challenges and triumphs of life, their bond growing stronger with each passing year.

As Sacha's story continues, his impact is felt far beyond the realms of music, nightlife, and sports. He becomes a respected figure in discussions on urban development, social policy, and community wellbeing. His insights and experiences are sought after by leaders and policymakers, and his opinion pieces and interviews are widely read and shared.

In his charitable work, Sacha's efforts contribute significantly to the well-being of countless individuals. His fundraising initiatives and advocacy work bring much-needed attention and resources to underrepresented causes. He becomes a symbol of hope and a source of inspiration for those striving to make a difference in their communities.

As Sacha Lord's legacy continues to unfold, his story is not just about the successes he has achieved but about the lives he has touched and the communities he has transformed. His journey is a reminder of the power of determination, the importance of innovation, and the impact of compassionate leadership. It is a narrative that resonates with those who dare to dream, those who strive to make a difference, and those who believe in the power of community. Sacha's story, woven into the fabric of society, continues to inspire and motivate, a lasting legacy of a life well-lived and a world positively changed.

Years roll on, and Sacha Lord's influence extends into the educational sphere. Recognizing the transformative power of education, he establishes a scholarship fund for underprivileged youth, focusing on those with a passion for the arts, music, and entrepreneurship. These scholarships provide opportunities for young talents who might otherwise be overlooked, offering them a platform to shine and contribute to the cultural and economic fabric of their communities.

Sacha's efforts in education don't stop at scholarships. He collaborates with universities and colleges, helping to develop courses that blend practical skills with creative innovation, preparing students for the rapidly evolving world of work. His lectures and workshops become highlights of the academic year, inspiring students to think outside the box and pursue their passions with vigor and determination.

In the political arena, Sacha's unbiased and pragmatic approach to problem-solving earns him respect across party lines. He is often called upon to mediate in complex negotiations, bridging gaps between differing viewpoints and finding common ground in seemingly irreconcilable differences. His knack for diplomacy and his unwavering commitment to the greater good make him a beloved figure in the political landscape.

As an author, Sacha pens a best-selling memoir, detailing his journey from a humble beginning to becoming a pivotal figure in various industries. His book becomes a source of inspiration for aspiring entrepreneurs and change-makers, offering valuable insights into the challenges and triumphs of pursuing one's dreams.

Printed in Great Britain
by Amazon

38044628R00030